"You will know the truth, and the truth will set you free." JOHN 8:32 NIV

Great is his faithfulness; his mercies begin afresh each morning. LAMENTATIONS 3:23 NLT

He redeems me from death and crowns me with love and tender mercies. He fills my life with good things. My youth is renewed like the eagle's! PSALM 103:4-5 NLT

He will cover you with his feathers. He will shelter you with his wings. His faithful promises are your armor and protection. PSALM 91:4 NLT

My God will meet all your needs according to the riches of his glory in Christ Jesus. PHILIPPIANS 4:19 NIV

"You will live in joy and peace. The mountains and hills will burst into song, and the trees of the field will clap their hands!" ISAIAH 55:12 NLT

To:

_____

From:

_____

Date:

_____

Library of Congress Cataloging-in-Publication Data

Names: Kavelaris, Amy, author.
Title: Good morning, little one : new mercies and prayers to carry you through the day / Amy Kavelaris.
Description: Nashville, Tennessee : Thomas Nelson, [2022] | Audience: Ages 4-8 | Summary: "Reassure kids that God is with them
    through the day with this good morning poem from Amy Kavelaris. Gorgeous animal flower-crown art and words of hope and
    blessing remind little ones of God's love, security, and peace for the day ahead"-- Provided by publisher.
Identifiers: LCCN 2021034584 (print) | LCCN 2021034585 (ebook) | ISBN 9781400231942 (hc) | ISBN 9781400231966
    (ebook)
Subjects: LCSH: Parents--Prayers and devotions. | Children--Religious life.
Classification: LCC BV283.C5 K38 2022 (print) | LCC BV283.C5 (ebook) | DDC 242/.645--dc23
LC record available at https://lccn.loc.gov/2021034584
LC ebook record available at https://lccn.loc.gov/2021034585

Written and illustrated by Amy Kavelaris

Printed in South Korea

22 23 24 25 26 SAM 6 5 4 3 2 1

Mfr: SAM / Seoul, South Korea / January 2022 / PO #12068556

To Mom and Pop:

My gratitude is *eternal* for your steadfast pursuit

of pointing me to the Lamb of God.

Love you forever.

To my dear readers:

May you seek and find Him everywhere.

His truth will set you free!

You are loved *beyond* description.

1 John 3:1 NIV

Hello there, precious little one.
It's time to rise and shine.
The day greets us with *fresh new hope*—
Oh, I'm so glad you're mine!

Lamentations 3:23

As you **wake** and **stretch** and *smile*,
The sunlight's streaming rays
Fill my heart with trust that God
Will *carry* you today.

Isaiah 46:4

He always keeps His promises.

He's written them all down.

He'll stay nearby to give you strength.

His *love* will be *your crown*.

Psalm
103:4–5

He'll pick you up when you get tired,

Protect you from the rain.

He'll *seek* and *find* you when you're lost.

He calls you by your name!

Not only does God carry you;

He's everywhere, you'll see!

Search for Him, both high and low.

His truth will set you free.

Perhaps you'll find a feather where
The seashore meets the tide—

Reminding you, beneath God's wings
You're *safest* by His side.

And when the spring rain whispers,
"Wake up" to sleeping seeds,

Remember God gives all His sprouts

Exactly what they need.

Philippians
4:19

Then skip and dance among the trees
And *worship* God in song.

The wind will join in *harmony*,
And leaves will clap along!

Just like a waterfall delights
In pouring past its brim,
Your *joy* from God will bubble up
And *overflow* from Him!

God hears your bold, excited prayers.
He hears your whispered call.
He loves to hear your special thoughts.
He made you, after all.

Psalm 139:2, 13–14

Should shadows fall and crowd your steps,

Big feelings squeeze you tight,

Know that in the darkness, child,

His love will *shine* most bright.

And as you shine your light for Him,
Our God rejoices too!
How beautiful that sound must be
When God sings over you.

I'm comforted the moment when

I send you on your way

That God reminds me *He'll be there*
Each minute of your day.

So as the morning dawns, sweet one,
Remember this—it's true!
Trust that you can count on Him.
Our God will carry you.

Isaiah 40:11

May the God of hope fill you with all joy and peace as you trust in him, so that you may overflow with hope by the power of the Holy Spirit. ROMANS 15:13 NIV

You know when I sit down or stand up. You know my thoughts even when I'm far away. . . . You made all the delicate, inner parts of my body and knit me together in my mother's womb. Thank you for making me so wonderfully complex! Your workmanship is marvelous—how well I know it. PSALM 139:2, 13-14 NLT

He will feed his flock like a shepherd. He will carry the lambs in his arms, holding them close to his heart. He will gently lead the mother sheep with their young. ISAIAH 40:11 NLT

"Surely I am with you always, to the very end of the age." MATTHEW 28:20 NIV